The Quickening Light

The Quickening Light

Poems by

June Blumenson

© 2023 June Blumenson. All rights reserved.
This material may not be reproduced in any form, published,
reprinted, recorded, performed, broadcast,
rewritten or redistributed without
the explicit permission of June Blumenson.
All such actions are strictly prohibited by law.

Cover design by Shay Culligan
Cover image by Raimond Klavins

ISBN: 978-1-63980-261-6

Kelsay Books
502 South 1040 East, A-119
American Fork, Utah 84003
Kelsaybooks.com

For Nick
The man in the Blue Shirt

Acknowledgments

With appreciation to the editors of the following journals for previous publication of poems and to Karen Kelsay and Delisa Hargrove at Kelsay Books for publishing and editing this second collection. And thanks to poets Ted Bowman, Sharon Chmielarz, Diane Jarvenpa and Tim Nolan for their generous reviews.

Adanna Literary Journal: Love Poems: "Say It," "Stealing Apples"
Avalon Literary Review: "Verboten"
Comstock Review: "Russian Vines," "Blue Shirt," "Death Scape"
Intimate Landscapes: Open to Interpretation: "Crossing"
Loft Literary Center/Minneapolis Institute of Art Sacred Short Award: "Dogs of War" (Installed at MIA)
Martin Lake Journal: "Circle of Black Mourning"
Masque & Spectacle Literary Journal: "Old Woman Leans Against Old Man"
The Moccasin: "The Devil's Come to Get Me," "Ablutions"
Nimrod International Journal, Finalist Pablo Neruda Prize for Poetry: "Making Soup with Neruda," "Words for Full"
Pomme Journal: "Side by Side"
Red Wing Arts 21st Annual Poet Artist Collaboration Chapbook: "Fugitive Color"
The Sandcutters: Journal of Arizona State Poetry Society Award: "A Thousand Horses," "Dogs of War"
San Pedro River Review: Back Roads & Byways: "Lodged in My Mind"
Southwest Journal: "Ascension"
SPANK the CARP: "Everything Is Fragile," "Swallowing the Mountain"
When Time and Space Conspire: "Voodoo in Cartagena"
Whistling Shade: "A Sparrow," "Connected"

Contents

I

The Quickening Light	15
What a World	16
Birth Record	17
Words for Full	18
Making Soup with Neruda	19
Ode to Neruda	20
Dance Lesson	21
Side by Side	22
Blue Shirt	23
Ablutions	24
Poetry Is an Egg	25
Old Woman Rests Against Old Man	26
Happiness	27
When Heads Roll	28
Lava Fields	29
Lifeline	30
Hummingbird	31
Thesaurus	32
Swallowing the Mountain	33

II

When the Lake Is Flat	37
At Large	38
A Child Asked, "What Is War?"	39
Before I Knew	40
Dogs of War	41
Daily Bulletin	42
The day the sky chased us	43
Me and My Shadow	44
In Search of Lost Time	45

Seven Deadly Sins	46
Fugitive Color	47
Evidence of Being	48
Thin Skin	49
I'll Never Tire	50
Falcon on My Wrist	51
The Far Side	52
Save the Day	53
Sparrow	54
Tick-Tock	55

III

A Thousand Horses	59
Stealing Apples	60
In Medias Res	61
Say It	62
Voodoo in Cartagena	63
Menage à Trois	64
Dama de Noche	65
In Search of Crumbs	66
Greyhound	67
november	68
Orange Light	69
Connected	70
Lean Against the Sky	71
Crossings	72
Intermezzo	73
words	74
Ascension	75
Lodged in My Mind	76

IV

We Have Lived Long	81
What She Knew	82
Verboten	83
The Elephant in the Room	84
Phone Call	85
Russian Vines	86
The Devil's Come to Get Me	87
Backstage Mom	88
Dollhouse	89
Circle of Black Mourning	90
Death Scape	91
Roots	92
This Old Tree	93
Race with the Sun	94
The Shore	95
Reflections from a Bridge in Venice	96
Shoot Me to the Stars	97

I

The Quickening Light

It's a kind of intimacy the way
he stares into my eyes
as if he can read my thoughts
deep beyond the retina. Alone
with him in a dim-lit room,
I strain to read the chart.
He measures the sharpness
of my vision, searches for a lazy eye.

There's a sense of apprehension
when he flashes lights to determine
blind spots, covers one eye at a time
to detect misalignment and fixation.

He flips lenses through varying degrees
of magnitude, checks for color
blindness, assesses depth perception.

In the end, my deficiencies
may be redeemable. We can fine tune
the lens power. It's a matter
of how I choose to see
the world in the quickening light.

What a World

According to a story
when the world
was created

it was spring
eternal yet lonely
immortal man gave

a rib from wounded
flesh to issue
a companion.

So many rules she said
no talking to
snakes in the grass,

no eating apples,
one bite,
banished,

then hand in hand
at a loss they
made their

solitary way
out of the delicious
garden into

encroaching darkness,
fully human, the imperfect
world before them.

Birth Record

Unlike Athena, sprouted fully-grown
from her father's head, born brave,
ready to take on challenges at birth,
I was conceived in the usual way

of two humans. A crybaby.
The last of six siblings, not
my parents' midsummer night dream.
They named me June.

I would have named myself Solstice
or Horizon, born on the cusp of Gemini
and Cancer, but it was not the dawning

of flowers and light. The whole world
was festering. Armored tanks roiled
across nations. Battle cries rang in the night.

Unlike Athena, I don't weave tapestries
depicting gods punishing mortals.
I'm not a virgin. I've never carried
a spear nor lived on top of a mountain.

And yet, like Athena, I was born in
an extraordinary way—nurtured
in a mortal mother's womb, dropped
into the birth canal, crowned at the vaginal
opening and pushed headfirst into the unknown.

Words for Full

I wait until the middle of May to fill the window
boxes, when there'll be no more frost, jonquils
replete, and tulips open like a woman

spreading her legs for love. I plant after all that
and just before bursts of purple sweet-rocket,
scarlet bells, and oh, my god, orange poppies,

one look at them, I'm in an opium den. An addict,
I spend a bundle at the nursery, overload the cart,
gorge myself with fusillades of color, oblivious

to zone or sun or shade, intense spikes,
everything teeming, spilling over. I know greed
breeds crowding, clutter, bound roots and early

seeding. I should plant smaller things, nurture
fragile seedlings, trust things will grow,
but I want everything now, satiate, summer.

Making Soup with Neruda

The dry parchment cracks and crumbles
like an ancient scroll, and a sweet sting
releases as I slice the onion
and throw it into the simmering stock.

Neruda sits, like the Buddha,
at my granite counter, watches me
shave the red stubble
from carrots, dice potatoes.

I serve him wine and tapas, holy
oblations of olives, rice-stuffed peppers,
goat cheese empanadas.
He tells me, voice rich as custard,
there is no such thing as a trivial tomato
or an ill-skirted cabbage. My eyes tear
from the roasted chillies
as we celebrate, my ordinary life.
I lend him my ruffled apron.

We mince garlic, scoop pumpkin,
pull strings from green beans.
All fall into the storm-tossed sea.
We wait for the vegetables to soften.

I take my best bone china
from the cupboard. So deeply,
I want to please him, afraid
flavors are lost in translation.
I ladle the carbonada, and Neruda pours
the moon into the white-jade tureen.

Ode to Neruda

My Pablo, I glow at the thought of you.
I know, if you were here, you'd love me—
my small potato-ness. You'd give me
your tender ear even as I disappear
into the big barrel of you. I love your socks,

your suit, the truth of you; how you grasp
the fragrance of cordwood, the rind
of a lemon; the deep well of you
that loves the cactus with its soft heart.

I love your sorrow for a child on the side
of the road peddling the death of a hare
to survive—your rage for the caged
pantera. Who said writers end up alone?
There. There you are, rain singing.

Dance Lesson

I was born to dance the Cuban
bolero, flirt with Argentine
tango. One two three four
cinco hold—cross left—*ocho*.

He calls himself El Toro. I lean
into his chest and he yells, *Commit,
commit, commit. Your weight
can only be on one foot or the other.*

I'm looking good in the arms
of El Toro. He puffs up like a rooster.
Switch. He shouts. *It's milonga.
Even if your woman has never

danced before, I'll always get
more from her than of you. Why?
Because I'm intentional.* I blush
as if I've swallowed a ripe
habañero. Men smolder.

I was born to dance in a skin-tight
dress with a long train of ruffle.
Unfurl. Eat mango. Fandango.
One two three four
cinco hold—cross left—*ocho*.

Side by Side

Love is a choice: 30 Ways to Love in Action
—Tiny Buddha

Today,
I have decided
to love
you.

When you
come home
and find me
on the balcony,

I will say,
hi, sweetheart,
pour yourself a glass of wine
and join me.

We
will sit in the sunshine,
watch
the black-capped chickadees
light on the railing,

bodies so small
I see their hearts lift,
so close
puffs of breath warm
my hand.

Like them we will sit
side by side
in the spring.

Blue Shirt

He waters the garden as if he's a high
priest of rain dousing the heads
of his supplicants. For where
would flat beans, squash, and kale
be without his benediction.

From inside the kitchen window,
I see him in his blue shirt, straw hat,
harvesting herbs. Last week
when he was packing for a trip,
he came and sat on the edge
of our bed. *I'll miss you,* he said,
and kissed my forehead.

*What exactly will you miss? Name
one thing,* I teased. *Now,* he said,
*seeing you softly tucked in, reading
in bed.* This is what we'll remember—

a blue shirt, a handful of thyme,
reading by the lamplight, my hair spread
on the pillow, when the winds of winter
press against the windows, and meager
is the season that once was so green.

Ablutions

I take my face
in my hands,
stroke
hollows there,
fingertips
brushing against
eyes, lips
throat,
breast,
down to
my soft belly,
washing
over dreams
wrapped tight
like buds
on the north side
of deep.
I sing lullabies
to the unborn,
lay in sweet wait
for dawn,
stretch,
search,
inside me the sun.

Poetry Is an Egg

with a horse inside
writes an anonymous

third grader, who gallops
a neck ahead of the pack.

Ah, the foal of it cracks
out of its shell, eyes

wide open. It lifts its head,
finds its spindly legs,

noses into walls and corners.
When grogginess lifts,

it trots to the edge
of a stream to drink,

then canters through
a clover field.

Ah, the free-rein of it.
A wild thing lengthens

its stride. Mane and tail
ripple in the wind.

Old Woman Rests Against Old Man

Vigeland Sculpture Park, Oslo, Norway

A whole garden of stone.
I want to run my fingers
over the rock-faces of an old
man and woman embracing.

They look as if they could crack
with longing, hungry for touch.

I will be like this someday.

But for now, the cold stone warms
in the sun, and these mammoth
creatures loom like gods
forging the human spirit immeasurable.

Happiness

So, I said to a friend when she opened her door to greet me, "Wow, you have such a beautiful smile, too bad you can't see it for yourself right now." And that got me thinking, how we smile at friends, strangers, gush over babies and dogs, but we don't smile at ourselves. I mean, that would be weird, right, to wake up, look in the mirror, smile and say, "Hey, morning, Sunshine." But why not? So I set out to smile more often, at myself. Every time I caught a glimpse in a storefront window, I mustered a wide grin. Before I knew it, I was smiling at my socks, my toothbrush, the refrigerator. I got so happy I thought I was getting taller, as if a golden thread was attached to the crown of my head and I unfurled, happiness snapping my shoulders back, stretching me upright, each vertebrae stacked one upon the other, like a column of building blocks reaching for the sky.

When Heads Roll

I was dusting the shelf, a wide swath
of inattention, when I knocked
the statue of Buddha from its mudra
of serenity. The head rolled across
the hardwood floor, bounced
to a stop an inch from the front door.

Buddha knew no fear, as if ready
for a swift Samurai sword to sever
head from torso, no cry of pain,
not even a sigh of surrender as when
Gandhi at his assassination uttered Om.

It was a clean cut. Perhaps I'd solved
the koan—killed the perfect
Buddha on the road. I knew
it was a lesson, but what teaching,
this piercing, this giving, this taking.

I cupped Buddha's head in my hands,
caressed it to my breast, glued it back
onto its body. If you look closely,
you will notice a hairline repair,
gladness, seamless imperfection.

Lava Fields

Small puffs of geothermal steam
percolate in the treeless landscape,

swirl like the first breath
of baby dragons. Proof—

life can happen anywhere. At any
moment, anything can give birth.

Lifeline

It was one of those late-winter mornings
as I drove to work waiting for the heat
to kick in when the rare occurrence
of traffic moved like a conveyer belt,
and swept me up in a steady flow.

Four hours shy of high noon, the sun,
harsh, colorless, consuming itself,
rebounded off banks of snow, paled
everything, and dared me to return its gaze.

I looked away. Pulled at the visor,
almost veered off the road to avoid
potholes when suddenly, I was overcome
with compassion for the burned
and washed out parts of life,

and I thought that's my sun up there,
laying claim to my lifeline, that streams down
on my planet, warms my hands on the steering
wheel and promises to last my lifetime.

Hummingbird

fattens up
for migration,
harvests insects
in flight,
thrusts
bill-shaped
tongue
into the nectar,

dart and drink
dart and drink

restless like this
sucks and sways,
swallows
the name
of each flower,
then flies away.

Thesaurus

Is there a synonym to describe
the semblance of solitude this morning
or a word for the way the darkness
withdraws to let early light touch the water?

Is there a word for the contradiction
between the fullness of peace and emptiness
of quiet? It's so calm, I could die here,
born again in the likeness of a kingfisher
bred in a nest floating on a halcyon sea.

Swallowing the Mountain

On
the seventh
day, I wanted
to slip into the city
of myself, away from
the constant expanse of big
sky, away from the super-sized
slopes of snow that rose to meet me.
I wanted to hide from the huge land, curl
into the safe cave of myself, retreat into the
folly of my fears, but my body, filled up with
the immense landscape, wouldn't bend in its usual
ways, would not let me, ever again, be as small as I was.

II

When the Lake Is Flat

Sometime when the lake is flat
and not even a stone
thrown causes a ripple, ask
how much you have loved
this world. Ask
if you would do everything

again and how deep your roots
dig into this ragged earth, and if,
spring's cracking ice-floes lift
your spirits. Ask how many
times you have gone under
the heave of swells
in distant storms of the past.

We come to the north shore
of the great lake. It could take
its pleasure of us in a heartbeat,
wingbeats of gulls circling above.

Everything is fragile.

At Large

I like early morning when the sky
is pale, and a quiet breeze billows
the curtains through an open screen.
Soon enough the sun will burn-off
fog to sharpen the day and foment
outrage at a world at large,
my small injustices laughable.

What's wrong with people, we ask,
meaning, *the other.* If only we were
strong enough to breach the divide.
But reaching out comes hard
like ripe apples pelting the earth
in the fall and nations turn
within themselves, as if, there is
an unquenchable appetite for sorrow.

A Child Asked, "What Is War?"

How could I name it?
Should I have said it is like grass,
familiar, a summer blade
mowed down, a buzzard's hymn,
the sea roiling? But she was five

and rocking on my lap. Her fingers
reached up, wound round my hair.
*Is it children who don't have food
to eat,* she asked, *lost cats
and dogs, the flowers gone?*

I did not know she knew these things
so well. How long would I hold her,
legs sun-kissed and growing,
her head against my shoulder.

That night when she lay down
to sleep, my heart gripped with fear.
Had she caught a glimpse
of nightly news, cats and dogs astray
in rubble, hollow-eyed children?
What song we sing? Ourselves.
Where are the leaves of grass?

Before I Knew

for George Floyd

Before I knew of broken treaties
and appropriations, I was a child
who grew up surrounded by reservations,
lived an uninformed life of convivial

thanksgiving. I dressed-up as Sacagawea
or Pocahontas for Halloween costumes.
My brothers played cowboys and Indians,
slept in tipis, tied each other to trees.

Before I knew of chains and lynchings,
that blood of slaves founded the wealth
of our nation, I believed in the happy
slave, Uncle Remus, plantation folklore,
the brotherhood of rabbits, bears, and foxes.

I watched Little Rascals, three-D movies
of Africans throwing spears into our popcorn.
Boys scanned National Geographic for pictures
of naked tribal women. And later,

when I lived through protests, assassinations,
Black is Beautiful, civil rights legislation,
I thought daylight had come
despite the confederate flag still waving,

despite statues and monuments glorifying
their affronts, despite mounting
evidence that denies all breath is equal.

Dogs of War

War is a failure of the imagination.
—Adrienne Rich

Who will come to honor the warriors when they are
fully steeped in darkness? Who will tear apart the earth
to reveal the names of some/one
on bracelets of war?
Dog-tags: pieces
of steel that over
simplify a life.
Tags: the price
to pay; a short
phrase attached to
a complete sentence;
the end of something;
a variation in the last
section of a song.
Who will go inside the heart
of monuments to carve out
the wounds of war? Tag:
to stamp as a work
of art for auction; to mark: as in
the images we take with us as we walk
away. Tag: what later we wish we'd said.

Author's Note: Poem is in response to Do-Ho Suh's sculpture, *Some/One,* made of thousands of military dog tags to form the silhouette of a traditional Korean robe. Broadside of poem installed near sculpture in Minneapolis Institute of Arts.

Daily Bulletin

As of December 2021, 693 cases fit the Mass Shooting Tracker project criterion in the U.S., leaving 703 dead and 2,842 injured.

Retired, he thought he'd seen it all—daily
bulletins flashing footage of bodybags
of boys he knew, hospital scenes
of Aids victims, and girls, who once
skipped rope, now women breaking
glass ceilings. He'd airbrushed
their faces from babies to wedding
celebrations, sold parents packets
of 2x3's and larger prints for the mantel.

But yesterday, his teenage grandson
sent him a message. *This school is next*
was scrawled on a mirror in the boys'
bathroom. He tries to quell his fears,
his memories downsizing.

He rifles through old photographs, finds
a classroom shot of his grandson's
kindergarten graduation. Pony-tailed
girls stretch up on tip-toes, the better
to see the world. His grandson stands
with other pint-sized boys, bursting
for independence, hoping for a future.

The day the sky chased us

we were sunning on a city park bench,
bluegills jumping at the slightest drop
of line in the overstocked canal.
A father shouted *basta* to his rowdy boys.
A woman tethered her daughter's coloring
book with a thermos as breezes grew.

Then the sky turned green. Gusts of wind
tossed paper plates and cups and a baseball
cap into the water. Dark clouds rolled in.
The temperature dropped. Sirens blew.

Everyone grabbed their things and fled
to the parking lot. A tailgating wall-cloud
churned as we clenched the wheel.
Straight-line winds advanced; debris
swirled around us. Sleeting rain poured
down as we pulled into our driveway
and made a bee-line to the basement.
Hail bulleted our faces. Afterward,

we sat dazed on the front steps, power
lines arced on the lawn, our sixty-foot
pine down, the neighbor's roof half gone—
stunned at how disasters chase us. And what
of the father and his playful boys, the mother
and her daughter who'd colored the sky blue?

Me and My Shadow

March 18, 2020 Pandemic

They look as if they're about to spring
through windows—mannequins,
dressed in trending 2020 colors,
optimistic, herbaceous,
and for the sartorial, bold flame
scarlet. It's a deserted village scene
during the coronavirus pandemic.
Still-life storefronts cast long shadows.
A dinner table in the corner kitchen
shop, replete with empty
napkin rings, soundless bell,
looks as if a family fled in a hurry.
The movie marquee is blank,
a hair salon boarded-up, an open Bible
in the window of the Christian Scientist
Monitor Reading Room reveals a passage
promising boundless light. *Food to Go!*
announces a restaurant sign but no one
is on the go except at the sporting goods
store, shielded behind tempered glass,
mannequins in baseball caps
and performance shoes jog in place.

In Search of Lost Time

Early days of 2020 Pandemic

There's a certain rhythm to my days,
maybe an underlying rhyme or two,
yes, definitely, a fundamental fragile
hum as I monitor my whereabouts,
regiment daily tasks. I hardly ever know
what day it is, have taken to color-coding
my clothing. Blue Monday, white
on Friday, to ensure, as in some cultures,
happiness will permeate the day.

Quarantined to reflection, I read a graphic
adaptation of Proust, can't quite grasp
his privilege, but, ah, the beautiful drawings,
the poetic text floating in thought-bubbles
above young Marcel's head. I fancy
a stroll by the lilies of Vivonne, a walk
in gardens of Combray, empathize
with his Aunt Leone sequestered
in her room with only the street to distract
her, musing about people who pass by.

I ponder *la madeleine* and yearn for a bite
of my mother's sweet-dough biscuits
baked in rich cream. Recall pastoral
summer days on my cousin's farm,
the horses' salt-block she dared me to lick,
the lost game of childhood when we pressed
our sweaty palms on a tabletop,
and to our astonishment, it began to rise.
In my garden, wafts of honeysuckle surround
me, a birdsong, a *little phrase,* a caress.

Seven Deadly Sins

2020 Pandemic

Plenty of time in this purgatorial place
to atone my misguided ways or commit
new transgressions—obsessive jabbering
on the phone, self-absorption, indignation
against restrictions, hankering after
what others have and languid days dull
as doorknobs, un-sharpened pencils.
What if this is forever?

Plenty of now during this scourge
of compromised living sidelined
to reflect on stockpiled memories,
hoard little mercies. I want, I want,
I want to grab a hand, take an unhindered
breath, stroll unmasked arm-in-arm
with a friend. I straddle sin and virtue.

Teeter. Totter. Try to focus on gratitude,
diligence, patience—then I'm junk.
Binge-watch through the night, raid
the wine cellar, long for the slightest touch.

Trapped in this prison of prolonged
now, I appeal for a reprieve from my puny
sorrows, try to hold onto some
semblance of grace   fleeting as a cloud.

Fugitive Color

A pigment that, when exposed to certain conditions
such as sunlight or temperature is less permanent.

I stroll through exhibits, but skies
do not break open with meaning.
No Large Blue Horses pound the earth,
no fount springs forth to reveal
significance. I sit at The South Ledges,
Appledore, the water's edge, the ledge
of jagged rocks, and stare out to sea.

I medicate on Oriental Poppies,
blood-orange as the moon,
so like a woman, like O'Keeffe,
who proved she could paint dark and muddy
like a man. I become the shimmering lover
held eternal in The Kiss. I am Chagall's
Poet Reclining. I am a Russian artist
reincarnate, Nikolai Aleksandrovich
Yaroshenko. Wet on wet,
I am Chandonnet, Canoeing in the Rain.

From words to canvas, chiseled
stone, layered pigment to page and ink,
I drift as if in a Jungian dream
where I am everything mirrored
in Atget's storefront windows,
reflecting random shadows,
plotless, errant shapes, fugitive color.

Evidence of Being

A goat
ate my camera in Goa,
leaving no proof of being.
Now you do not believe me
when I tell you,
I saw mermaids,
sea angels that they were,
fanning the flaming sun
with their fins,
as it sank into the sea,
the Arabian Sea,
the swallowing sea.

Steam rose—
when the sun hit the water,
and I heard
a searing sound
that broke the silence
in Goa.

A goat
ate my camera in Goa.
Now when you ask me,
where do you come from,
I cannot tell you.
There is no trace
or trail to here,
there is only my body,
bearing down hard
against the earth,
that may leave
no proof of meaning.

Thin Skin

Someday, my friends and I laugh,
we'll no longer want to be on top
during sex, jowls hopelessly slack,
breasts sagging down to our bellies,
love gone dark and undercover.

Will we tip-toe to spas, roll in mud
like elephants driven to shade
and shallows, massage the menacing
complexities of age that breakdown
the subcutaneous layer of skin—
the dermis no longer connective?

Will our losses render us invisible—
unlovable—the epidermis stretched
papery thin, sensitive to light,
and hungry for the slightest touch?

I'll Never Tire

of being a woman. When I walk
into a flower shop, a department
store, the bakery on the corner,
I rise like yeast in a warm oven.

I'm an escalator going up. I want
to lie down in a spa, let hot stones
walk over my body. I'm a bath brimful.
I love my feet, painted nails, my hair,

the mystery of dark shadows under my eyes.
I love being a woman. I want to go on
forever like a comet of light, sheer ballast
stretched out, streaking happiness across

the sky. I stroll around the lake, my eyes,
my shoes, my joy memorizing everything.
I walk through parks, pass the hardware
store, eat gelato in the ice-cream parlor

courtyard, even when it's drizzly cold,
the fire pit burning, my feet up on the grate
warming, magnolia petals, cherry blossoms
swirling like snow flakes in April wind.

Falcon on My Wrist

When I am old,
I will carry a falcon
on my wrist, sip
English tea, naked
beneath my skirt,
free from false starts
and labored births,
when demands are few
and no matter what I do,
I'll be deemed
wonderful, wise,
an everlasting
monument to low
expectations.
A flip of the wrist
the falcon
unrestrained,
will fly hither
and beyond the sea,
the rainbow,
the white cliffs
of everywhere,
and from the farthest
point with its great
power of sight,
will change direction
rapidly and dive
at impossible speed
to devour me.

The Far Side

When the alarm tears
through the dawn,
through marshlands
of sleep, I make a fist
and punch time,
try to crawl my way back
into dreams unnoticed,
steal into a roomful
of people, grope along
walls while everyone sees
right through me, knows
I no longer belong.
I squeeze my eyes shut
against filtering light,
yearn to stay just long
enough to claim my lump
of soul shed somewhere
in that bottomless place,
but sleep, ready to clear
her heavy throat, lifts
her shroud and casts me
out into the morning.

Save the Day

It just dawned on me
that I need to reset
my clocks. Do I fall back,
leap forward into the unknown?
I struggle to fall asleep,
then wake during the night.
My brainwaves lag
and I want to stay in bed
all morning. I suspect
I'm a moonflower, more likely,
a bat. The longer the days
become the more I lurch
forward, my circadian
rhythm out of whack.
Only a white man can cut
the top off a blanket
and call it longer, a wise
Indian said. The shorter
days become, the more
I slip into darkness,
my biological clock confused.
Elsewhere, the sun rising.

Sparrow

lights on my windowsill,
calm, definitive.

I think its eyes are on me
nesting under eiderdown,
unblinking into dawn's
lifting darkness. But it's only
pecking away at itself
in the rain-spotted glass.

Yesterday, someone I knew died.
We were two feathers brushing
against each other's cheek.

I pull the eiderdown closer
to my body. The sparrow
beats its wings—
whistles its two-second song.

Tick-Tock

As a child I mastered time, could read a face, was sentinel
of the hour. *The short hand is on twelve,* I said,
the long one on seven. Round and round time
revolved, minutes flew on a downward
spiral from one, two, three toward six,
then climbed-up past eleven. I liked
noon and midnight best, when as if
in prayer, the hands pressed
together. Before digital or
grandfather and atomic
clocks, pocket watches
and sundials, sticks
and bones tracked
phases of the moon.
And
even human
hands can predict
when the sun expires
so you find your way home
before lost in the wild. But enough
about old clocks and shadows, there
is talk of smoothing future wrinkles,
and some say even death is only a technical
problem. But what is the point of stretching the
strings of time or cracking the code of aging, if
there's no hope humankind will avert the planet's demise.
Time is a flicker of light, a leap of a year, a frog, a child.

III

A Thousand Horses

Words fly, unbridled
like a sudden gust of wind
and all the king's horses

can't retrieve them. No
rattling gourd or incantation
drives out the monster.

No long-tongued hound
licks the wound, and remorse,

unbroken, mounts a thousand
wild horses and cannot
make friends with the wind.

Stealing Apples

We were out stealing apples,
an autumn hike in the woods,
when he took an abrupt turn
away from the trail along the calm
side of the lake, away from canopies
of colored leaves, the flush of grouse,
away from me and the orange fox
who came out of the bushes
her face like mine, friendly
but not quite tame, my hot stare
pressed against his back
as he walked away steaming.

He took a shortcut
back toward the busy road,
dust and noise from steam shovels
digging, the smell of diesel,
the honk of horns, tired construction
workers resting on their shovels.

Then, as if to mock us, rescue seaplanes
roared on maneuvers overhead,
landing and taking off on the lake,
like the coming and going
of our love, a love
that sometimes walks on water.

I felt a surge of regret
we had not stuffed our pockets full
when we had the chance,
for lean times ahead
with the juiciest apples we had ever stolen.

In Medias Res

It stormed
in the night—not
exactly a blizzard
more like a biting rain
that left a sigh
frozen
on the window.
When you care
too much, the heart
falls like a stone
into a pond,
concentric circles
ripple around it
until they disappear,
and in the middle
of things
the heart goes still.

Say It

Because the season turned to fall, and flowers spent, drooped
their heads, emptied of everything they had to give,
he bought her sunflowers wrapped in cellophane
from the corner store,
as if translucent film could hold longevity, as if
their beaming faces could shed some light

on what it was he meant to say. In Victorian times,
the flowers would have spoken more clearly,
fortunes told by petals pulled,
one long hot breath upon the dandelion head and seeds
of the faithful dispatched,
the bluebell constant,
the purple columbine resolved,
a time when just the color of the chrysanthemum could signal
whether someone told the truth.

You have to learn to trust the seasons.
She knew this, still,
she wanted grieving marigolds or orchids that cannot hide
their easy bruise,
flowers of certitude that said, *I'm sorry* or *let's start again*
like one stem of lily of the valley
picked from a spring garden, but it was not the season.

Voodoo in Cartagena

I hadn't bargained for the shacks
along the tarmac at the airport,
or the air pressing like a death mask
when we deplaned.

Blackness everywhere transfixed me,
and the evening, crying for the moon,
held its breath in perfect stillness,
as if warning all to stay away.

I had a strange dream that thick night
that a child lay close beside me,
and when I woke, the heat
from the child's body slipped away.

It was then I heard the drumming,
could almost touch the intrigue,
saw myself running into the hard
sky, wild like someone gone mad.

Was it stories I'd heard of kidnappings
and bandits in the hills, or displaced African
tribes, free from bondage, rituals intact,
who live deep in the jungles? Was it drug

cartels, armed guerrillas or that tall, swarthy
man hitting on me as I sat in the outdoor cafe
late in the night drinking scotch and water?
Or was it the baggage I'd brought with me
to the impossible beach riled up like a desert storm?

Menage à Trois

He's a handsome man,
olive skin, a larger frame
than what she's used to,
carries his weight well.
Don't look now, she whispers
to her husband, *but doesn't
that man at the table behind
you resemble your cousin?*
She feigns a glance at his
scrumptious hors d'oeuvres.

His eyes catch hers and linger
past his companion's shoulder.
The chef sends a gratuitous
charcuterie platter. *Pâté,
jambon-de-bayonne.
Cornichons* for a hint of acid.
The c*hateaubriand* arrives.
Seared to perfection. *Bleu.*

Dama de Noche

I move differently here
in the jungle,
after a day in the hot
sun, hips tropical,
lips moist
as the rain forest,
skin warm
as chipotle, and eyes,
smoldering
like a volcano.

I take on the fragrance
of lemons,
flower like the Queen
of the Night,
swell and open
to the dusk,
close to the dawn.

I wear a long tiered
skirt, bright
as the scarlet macaw,
a scoop necked
blouse, blue
as the blue-crowned
motmot with one sleeve
lowered to reveal
my silken shoulder.

In Search of Crumbs

I looked back, like Gretel, saw my sole
in shreds, bits of crepe-lug scattered
like bread crumbs along the mountain slope,
marking my way back to the lodge where the cooks
roasted rack of lamb and wild salmon.

Wow, the trail is really beating up your boots,
our naturalist guide said. I kept going,
plunged my walking stick in the muck,
polluting the path with strange scat
for birds and bears to ponder.

In all their years of service, my boots
never once gave me a blister,
not when I sloshed waterproofed
through city streets against incessant rain,
or stubbed my toes on scree
and roots in the woods,
or picked a path through lava fields.

I never named these boots as some who name
their cars, as if to christen them
would protect me, keep me from losing my way.

Greyhound

What did we know of losing
our religion when we steeped
ourselves in poetry and other books
we barely understood—our half
read manifesto, *On the Road*.

What did we know when City
Lights beckoned us to the west
coast bay, when we rode the Greyhound
through the Bad Lands straight-on
to Billings and Nevada's blazing
sunsets where the driver stopped
at every one-armed bandit,
we got carded and the sheriff sent us
packing to the Happy Buddha Cafe.

We washed-up in seedy depots, ate junk,
and you snored upon my shoulder
but I didn't sleep for two days. Just stared
out the window until we coasted down
the hills of San Francisco. Two small-town
girls in the big city for a week of play.

What did I know of happenings
or dharma when I hopped
a streetcar to the bookstore in search
of "beatnik" sightings, so afraid
of myself, I journaled in code
I've forgotten how to decipher,
and innocence was just a throw-away.

november

because it was
november
and there was nothing

more to do
outdoors
leaves mulched

garden beds
at rest
snow fences

staked
to keep away
rabbits   and deer

she soaked
in a scented
bath, then sat

by the fire
to winter over
like a hothouse flower

no bones to pick
no water
to carry   not even

wood to split
tongues of fire   sealed
behind tempered glass

Orange Light

If you would join me
on an autumn day,
we'd crunch clusters
of wayward leaves,
watch people
come and go talking
of all their highs
and lows. I'd borrow
Oliver, you'd recite
Plath. We'd walk
three miles
around the lake,
speak of black pine-
trees in orange light.

Our words would land
in colorful trees
and cling
like decisions
until wind
blew them away.
We'd exchange
views, confide
revisions,
talking of all
our highs
and lows, wild geese,
and lovers
who come and go.

Connected

At first glance he appears
to be praying, a kind faced
man sitting on a park bench,
head bowed, downcast eyes,
hands cupped in silent meditation.

Then his thumbs twitter. Oh,
he's holding his phone.
Is he shopping for a right-now
bargain, addicted to instant news,
reading mail, checking weather?
Does he even notice the jogger
loping to keep up along side

his dog? Does he inhale the scent
of magnolias, hear lake waves
tease the shore? But who am I
to say, lost in my own thoughts,
making judgements. Ruining my day.

Lean Against the Sky

Later
I tried to think what I might have said
that would have been worthy of her pen,
when we ate cookie ice-cream, and she took
key notes while I talked as if I were famous.

I wanted to give her something.
Tell her to throw away unhappiness.
Instead, I picked up the tab, swept my words
like crumbs off the table, tiny specks
of succor fell to the floor.

Do what makes you happy, I wanted to say
as if I had answers. I wanted to shake her.

You don't have to wear a hair-shirt
or bloody your knees. Just hold
what is yours in your hands. Do what gives you
ten thousand joys, and yes, leaves you
with ten thousand sorrows after they're gone.
You are a mountain. Lean against the sky.

Crossings

Like a long pause between now
and then, suspended
beyond all understanding, we say
we'll cross that bridge when we come
to it leaning against fog-dropped skies
of uncertainty. I hardly register

the accumulation of crossings
each day, the faint intake
of breath, the exhalation, the precise
moment overtaken by sleep
or the flutter of eyelids in the morning,
until the passage of time, taut

as cables between portals,
its dead load susceptible
to wind, sways up, down
and sideways, and resonates
like a string plucked on a guitar.

Intermezzo

Massenet's Thais

It's amazing to be at the opera,
high definition live, the stars
pixel crisp, giants on the screen.

I could stand in Athanael's open
mouth, pan for gold on the skin
of Thais, caught in that common
pit of the people, eating popcorn,
rattling irreverence.

Then the long breath
of the intermezzo,
D major *Andante religioso,*
a hymn to sacred love.

It's as if I've been groping in the dark
forever and suddenly find something
I didn't know I'd lost; the harps,
the violin solo, *poco più appassionato,*
eros and agape on the silver screen.

words

we sit in the meditation   hall
each trapped   in our web
of story   how she said
he said   this   that   long

narratives that although   then
seem real   now   fists
close around   the shiniest
marbles   bursts of anger
the struggle   to be at ease

we take refuge   in the one seat
of silence   while the mind's
frenzied dance   tempts
the abyss   hoping our breath

provokes   wisdom
counting on   the generosity
of heart   to drop
words   at the doorstep

Ascension

It was only yesterday
I raked the spirals
of falling leaves,
colors of bruised
plums, bricks and amber.

Now this—
a world delicate as white
tea, rooftops thick
with cold, the bent
mugo pine, and snow angels

flat on their backs,
wings spread, searching
the night sky
as they disappear
under drifts
and fly-up to heaven

Lodged in My Mind

We boarded the train in the dark
the only landscape
our reflections fogged
in the steam of our breath
against the cold
sleeper-car window traveling
as if in an earlier century
like pilgrims to God's country.

When I woke the moonlight
had slipped into the morning sky
had slipped like a lie
into conversations had slipped
into my bones
brittle as Dakota winter.

I took my coffee in the club car
an aftertaste of seared
bison and beer from the night
before, journaled voluminous
omissions. Missing scenes.
The obliterate horizon.
I felt bizarrely orphaned as if
the mountain I carried inside me
had so diminished
it hardly resembled a small hill.

The train stopped at a concrete
platform somewhere between
the Blackfeet Reservation to the east
and the Flathead Reservation
to the west. The porter unloaded
our bags faster than the time
it took to whistle.

Moonlight flooded the timberline
cedars and a tall fortress
of spruce. The only evidence of life
was tracks, perhaps a wolverine
or lynx. Fossil country
where no dense areas of human
contingencies exist.

We trudged a half mile in the snow
to a country lodge to sleep
for the night. The immense
wilderness lodged in my mind.
In the morning, fits of sunlight
illuminated crystals blowing
like gold dust landing singular in trees.

IV

We Have Lived Long

In my grandmother's house,
where ancient grandfathers lusted
after harvest moons, wind blows in
through broken windows. A calendar
flutters on a rusty nail, losing track

of itself, trying to remember something
important, marking the separation
of generations. Everyone remembers

things differently or not at all,
and mildewed memories cause us to sneeze
at insignificant things we note.

Ancestral memories as our witness
we have lived long
against poor odds of survival.

We look around at those who are still with us,
try to guard against the day we will be
orphaned. We honor the empty spaces
like wolves that keeps a place
in the circle for those who are gone.

What She Knew

On my mother's bookshelves
were dusty volumes,
faded Britannica, bindings barely
broken. To read was a luxury
in her world. She'd made her unfair
bargain, traded books for dirty
dishes, piles of laundry,
impeccable floors. I wonder
when she dusted, did she
quickly swipe around the edges,
move each book aside
to wipe underneath?
Did she blow away specks
of grime that settled on spines
and gilded heads? Did her knotted
fingers hold each volume,
leaf through chapters to release
what was hiding there? My mother
didn't have time to read the books
that lined her shelves,
but oh, what she knew by heart.

Verboten

Ours was a house of stuffed things.
Cabbages. Sausages.
Closets. Chairs. Fried strudels
and boiled pockets of dough filled
with vegetables and spices. A meat
and potato house. Popovers, plump
with proof of the pudding. Throats
crammed with secrets. Suitcases
packed with pain. The dead
clammed up in eternity. Stuffed with soul.

Our house had laws, recipes for peace
keeping. Never sit on a made bed.
Never go barefoot. Dinner on time,
if you wanted to live on the buttered
side of our home. The pressure cooker's
whistle penetrates the silence, announces
it's about to explode in my mother's kitchen.
Pots on the stove blow off steam.

The Elephant in the Room

sits at the head of the table, apologies
for slurping soup from my bowl
at the other end—a long stretch
of its trunk—drips only a few drops
from bowl to mouth, mouth to bowl.

How is it no one else can see him, even
as my bowl empties and I haven't lifted
my spoon? More food! More food
we cram into our mouths. Wash
it down. Avoid secrets in the gravy.
The fork runs away with the spoon.

I want dinner to be over. The elephant
trumpets around the table. How is it
no one else can hear him, even as
he stands on hide legs and roars?

Phone Call

After the weather report and updates
of older brothers and sisters,
I pushed through the weak connection

and said it. *Am I crazy, Mom? I have no
memory of you when I was little—only a vague
sense of wandering an empty house.*

Silence pulsed through the landline's twisted
wires. She whispered, afraid my father
in the next room might overhear.

*Six kids. No education. I couldn't leave him.
I was so tired. I was . . . sleeping.* She began to cry.

Then, as if swept away by a flash flood
with its power to change everything,
I went under three times.
Saw what her life had been.
Resurfaced in the calm water
of compassion. Forgave her everything.

Russian Vines

On the dark side of the house, where shadows
shade the hosta and at every turn surprise,
my brother sits on his stone bench.
He knows the things we share—

how we romanticized our roots—the Steppe,
sunflowers, Dostoevsky, the Black Sea.
I wander along pebbled paths, remembering
secrets that twine like Russian vines fragrant

with racemes, and the tears he shed that day
when we saw the movie *Brokeback Mountain*.
I've already seen this film, he said, when we settled
in our seats, *but I want to see it again with you.*

My body shifted away from his. My face flushed
during the love scenes. I was glad for the darkness;
his tears so fresh it seemed like this was yesterday
for him. I understood, there, in the darkness, if that

is ever possible. I knew his loss, how hard and deep
secrets were planted and turned. The garden path
curves round, and I join him on his bench. Claim him,
tangled as we are. Hearts like bursts of bloom.

The Devil's Come to Get Me

I worked hard as a kid learning
to smoke, paired the sharp inhale
with chocolate, learned
to suck it up, swallow it down.
And now, Doctor, you scrape it out
of me, that cauliflower-shaped betrayal
of my former smokin' self,
a tumor the size of a pencil eraser.

I lit up like a movie star
on my way to college, stood
between the train's coupled passenger
and club car. Trench coat, sunglasses,
the bright burn of the cigarette tip
in the night, everyone was *looking at me,
kid.* The long, slow drag—something

to accompany my scotch and water,
my Ella Fitzgerald, my Ferlinghetti.
Then the habit took off like a lit fuse
to sneak into my morning coffee,
snaked through dessert and foreplay.

For years the blue haze softened
my vision, blurred the hard edges.
And now, Doctor, you say, new
tumors will grow back every few years,
the dark horseman hitching me
to the post and whispering, *hey, pony up.*

Backstage Mom

> . . . *She that had no need of me. . . . Lost in Hell,—*
> *Persephone . . .*
> —Edna St. Vincent Millay

I pop the car trunk, throw
her laundry bag over
my shoulder, obsessed
with some bit role
in my college daughter's life,
(as a laundress!) *There are no*
*small parts, only small actor*s.

I sort her soiled goods,
dirty socks and sour things,
her monthly blood,
Victoria's secrets, damp
towels mixed with work-out
sweat, mascara smeared
wash cloths. I hate this part.
I want to rerun nursery scenes,
gather up and rock the freshness
of her, sink my face
into flannel sheets, fold pastel
pull-on pants and footed sleepers.

I empty the dryer-tray lint,
stuff the soft clean clothes
back in the bag. I must let her go.
My winters will be long.

Dollhouse

I still see your face peering
into rooms of the dollhouse family,
child fingers placing tiny music
sheets on the baby grand piano,
a two-inch mom winding a dime
sized ball of yarn, the toy dad and girl
playing Go Fish at a small table.

I still feel your breath against my neck,
sense your choked-back tears,
and your confusion when you grabbed
the tall legs of your parents, pulling us
together, your face pressed against our knees.

What's divorce? you asked, then moved
the dollhouse dad outside to look
inside a window. You informed us,
*I know how babies are made, the woman
has the egg and the man has . . . the spirit?*

We'll never know the depth of hurt
our severance cost you. It was a shrunken
time. But you, daughter of broken
houses, grew a big heart and enlarge
our small world. You are the sky.

Circle of Black Mourning

You arrived at my door frail
and hungry. I could not read
your sunken eyes. I wanted
to hold you but the barrier
between us was too strong.
You, ravished by the rasp
of death. Me, on the other side,
wanting to restore you.
Did you appear in my dream
to tell me you are okay? Yes, yes,
I will watch over the daughter
we share. So many things
I did not say, my voice hoarse.
Caw, caw. It is not a beautiful
sound, clicks, rattling of bones.
I have seen a crow funeral, how
they fly in one by one. At first,
a peck, a nudge, to verify the dead
are really dead. Kraa, kraa.
They pronounce a passing. Slow
and graceful, rise dark as evening sky.

Death Scape

It could have been the rain
that woke me,
although it felt harsher, the startle
of grief for his unexpected death.

His sudden collapse like a sink hole,
a fracture in the air,
not a disappearance but a transformation
from firm ground to sunken
landscape or an ice-cube melting
in its own remains—from presence
to memory, from solidity to fluid.

There is less of him now
and his dissolution will continue
until the water runs clear
and when we drink, it will taste of gone.

Roots

After we stretched
our legs
three miles around
the lake,
we lazed
on the shallow
roots of a silver maple.

Junk trees
some people call them
because they are weak,
but I say,
junk is what's inside
us when we can't think
of a single song
on a summer day.

This Old Tree

The old maple stands in a stately yet sassy
pose, rear-end thrust out, arms raised
to the sky. It's become quite androgynous
over time, knots the size of breasts
and a burly phallus bulging below its waistline.

I've lived here for three decades of its eighty
years, witnessed the severance of branches
and limbs, pickup up its debris after storms,
raked its blood-red leafage each fall.
It has sheltered me during hard times.

I love this tree. I hug it even though its girth
is too huge for my arms to wrap around. I thank
the giant limbs for not killing me, for not even
damaging the roof. I think the tree knows me.
We've weathered together for so many years,
told each other everything in our quiet ways.

Race with the Sun

Just before twilight
when the sun is low in the sky
and casts a long shadow,

blue tones scatter,
and the color temperature
warms to a glow.

Some call it the golden hour
when a veil of magic hinges
on remaining slivers of light.

It's then there is a small window
of relief from the day's glare,
a last chance to focus a wide lens,

the sun at our back shooting out
a brilliance that renders us
softer than we've ever been.

The Shore

A man bends to investigate a tide-swept shell
on the rocky shore as the wind catches
the thump, thump percussion of a boy's ball
bouncing on rocks in sync with resounding waves.
No tall ships today, the small town relieved
of the spillage of city folk, crowds of tourists.

We arrived the day after the ships sailed.
Today, not even a fishing rig in view. The way
we like it, an emptiness that goes on forever,
as if at any moment, we could sail over
the thin line of the horizon where the world ends.

What would it be like to travel to the edge
of the earth where mythology exists, to fall
into a place where bare-breasted women glitter
with scales, to pratfall from the world's comic
stage, nose-dive into the unknown?

Is this what death feels like? Falling, falling,
falling. I once fell off my bicycle, backward
in slow motion. I couldn't believe I couldn't stop it,
that I wasn't in control. I lay on the trail, stunned.
Yes, that must be what death is—a suspension,
a surrender, an unbelievable time-stopped fall.

Reflections from a Bridge in Venice

Venice sinks almost an inch a year.

She is old now, mostly abandoned,
except for vendors who eke out a living
from the little she still has to give,
and strangers who come to stare
at her desperate face-lifts, to reconcile
tales of grandeur with the cracked
and lonely face that floats before them.

It was a noble life, the grand-dame muses,
shuttered up in her damp house with her
labyrinth of memories barnacled with saints,
masked balls, pearl-laden hazes of love
and kaleidoscopes of cut-glass remains.

In the stillness, she listens for the distant
clacking of tectonic plates under the sea
that rises more each day to taunt her,
and sinks another inch into the jade-green bath.

Shoot Me to the Stars

When I blow into hell,
I'll grab death by its horns,
somersault down the back
of that charging bull,
catapult into heaven and dance
with angels on the head of a pin.

There'll be banners strung
from star to star, planets
and moons twirling
like dervishes, comets wagging
their tails as the ever-so-coy
milky way drops her veil
to reveal the universe.

Only then will I give it a rest,
long enough to see
you are not pulling sad faces,
but hold me one last time
and delight as I shape shift,
no longer bound up in body,
free to laugh long into the night,
loud enough to wake the dead.

Do not cry for I have shed
enough tears to wash me out
beyond the sea somewhere
and burst the seams of life again.

Author's Notes and Influences

A Child Asked "What Is War": Walt Whitman, *Leaves of Grass, Songs of Myself*

Backstage Mom: Russian director, Konstantin Stanislavski remarked that "There are no small parts, only small actors."

Birth Record: James Wright, *A History of My Life*

Dogs of War: In response to Do-Ho Suh's sculpture, *Some/One*, made of thousands of military dog tags to form the silhouette of a traditional Korean robe

Fugitive Color: Franz Marc, *Large Blue Horses*; Childe Hassam, *The South Ledges, Appledore*; Georgia O'Keefe, *Oriental Poppies*; Gustav Klimt, *The Kiss*; Marc Chagall, *Poet Reclining*; *Self Portrait of Nikolai Aleksandrovich Yaroshenko*; Ann Chandonet, *Canoeing in the Rain: Poems for My Aleut Athabascanson*; Eugene Atget, photographs of Paris storefront windows

In Search of Lost Time: *In Search of Lost Time: Swann's Way, A Graphic Novel, Adaptation and Drawings* by Stephane Heuet, Translated by Arthur Goldhammer

Ode to Neruda: Referenced Neruda Odes: A Smell of Cordwood, Black Panthers, Boy with a Hare, Ode to an Artichoke, Ode to a Lemon

Orange Light: Referenced poems: T.S. Eliot, Love Song of J. Alford Prufrock; Sylvia Plath, Black Pine Tree in an Orange Light; Mary Oliver, Wild Geese

Thesaurus: Charles Simic, *The Dictionary*

When the Devil Comes to Get Me: Lisa Mueller, *Monet Refuses the Operation*

When the Lake Is Flat: William Stafford, *Ask Me*

About the Author

June Blumenson, author of *A Scythe of Moon* (2020), lives in Minneapolis, curates a poetry reading series, and facilitates poetry workshops. She is widely published in journals including *Boston Literary Magazine, San Pedro River Review,* and *The French Literary Review.* Her awards include Comstock Literary Review Award, Journal of Arizona State Poetry Society, The Poet's Billow Atlantis Award, Literal Latte Award, The Loft/Minneapolis Institute of Art Sacred Shorts Writing Contest Award, and Red Wing Arts 21st Annual Poet Artist Collaboration. She was a finalist for *Nimrod*'s Pablo Neruda Prize for Poetry. When asked why she writes, she likes to quote Kurt Vonnegut, "I write so that I can edit myself into some semblance of intelligence."

Special Thanks

to Sandra Kacher and Liz Weir for their friendship and editorial comments on final drafts; for insightful critiques from my brilliant writing group: Mary Junge, Shannon King, Sandra Larson and Carol Rucks; and for continued support from my Poetry Club cohorts and friends Colleen Cavell and Gretchen Pinsonneault. I am grateful for family and many friends who always show up. This book is for you.

www.ingramcontent.com/pod-product-compliance
Lightning Source LLC
Chambersburg PA
CBHW021328190426
43193CB00040B/777